The

M.A.P.

A Personal Guide for You on Your
Journey towards a Better Life!

Chester L. Hall Jr, M.Ed, CLC, CALC

A GOODLIFE!! Coaching Publication

Chester L. Hall Jr, M.Ed, CLC, CALC
 The M.A.P: A Personal Guide for You on Your
 Journey towards a Better Life!
 116 pp.
 ISBN-13: 978-0692571248

1. Self-Help   2. Personal Development
3. Life Coaching
I. Title

Copyediting by Lakishia Bannister
Page Layout & Design by Chester Hall
Cover Design by Chester Hall
Illustrations by Randy Glasbergen
 Glasbergen Cartoon Service
 E-mail: randy@glasbergen.com
 Web: http://www.glasbergen.com

Table of Contents

Dedication

A few years ago, my wife and I reflected back over the events and friends we've encountered in our lives so far. At that time, it seemed like everyone we knew was writing a book of some sort on life reflection and becoming "liberated" in the process. We both looked at each other and said, "What does writing a book have to do with moving your life forward?" Well baby, I've been liberated! Here's my book as proof!

I am dedicating The M.A.P. to my wife and best friend, Nyoka "Nye" Charlene Hall, because she has helped me immensely in becoming the individual I am today. My mother and father did a tremendous job instilling morality, values, a strong work ethic, and showing me how to care for others more than myself; ultimately raising me to become the man that Nye would want to marry. As my partner, she has upheld and exceeded the vows of marriage by leaps and bounds, aiding me in becoming the man that I wanted to be, just like how this book will aide you in becoming the person you want to be.

You never really know who you are until you have a good woman by your side to show you what you're really made of. She has stood with me through good and bad, thick and thin, and when I didn't know which direction I was headed in, she became my compass. She is my rock.

This past August, we celebrated 12 years together as a married couple, but 20 years in total as best friends. I can't think of a better way to show my gratitude for her vesting in me than by dedicating this book to her. Thank you and I Love You!

Ched

Foreword

Are you looking for a good place to start to make major changes in your life? Have you found many self-help books are just too comprehensive to digest? Are you ready to start your major "life change" now? If the answer is "YES", then The M.A.P. is the right book to supplement your journey.

As a visionary leadership trainer, inspiration teacher, pastor and seminar sponsor, I have found the content of this "How To" book to be a "Must Read" for people who are seriously committed to taking their lives into another dimension.   This book is also a "Must Read" for anyone who needs a place to start towards massive productivity or those who desire to up their game. I have lead people in some capacity for over forty years. My personal experience has been that many people know that they need change. The question is "HOW?"

The author, Chester Hall, has spent his entire life developing himself and others around him. He has taken the wisdom and strategies obtained through studying and practical experience and placed it in an easy-to-read book. Topics such as vision, goals, self-discipline and team-building are covered on the pages of this literary work. It is full of definitions, instructions, strategies, illustrations, examples, worksheets, and assignments.   Reading this book will not only inspire you, but it will move you to take action. Chester uses very simplistic language and relatable imagery to motivate the reader to take the steps needed for change.   If you are ready to submit to the process, The M.A.P. can get you to the destination.

David A. Sabatino, BS in Technology Education
Founder: Inspire & Empower
Pastor: Foundation of Faith Ministries
Inspirational Teacher/Speaker
Belle Haven, Virginia

Hey! How's everything? Can you meet later today? The weather is better.

Good...I'm not at home. I'm spending some quality time with my friend for the weekend. We're actually heading out in a few.

👍 Good stuff! I'll get with you later next week...I think you're almost where you want to be. Enjoy!

I'm starting the Health part of my "pie" Monday. I'm gonna set myself a 3 month goal and I know I can do it!

Of course you can! Do you see how getting one part of your life together raises the bar for everything else? This is great! Don't mind me anymore...we will talk next week. Have a good time!

Okay and Chester, I really want you to know that you have been a blessing in my life, because I honestly wouldn't be pursuing any of my dreams without your encouragement.

Awesome! You had it in you the whole time...I just gave you a push! Now stop talking to me. 🙂

A Brief Conversation via Facebook Messenger with client and friend Y.W. (October 2015)

Introduction

Welcome to **The M.A.P.** My name is Chester, and I will be your guide during this adventure in building your new life by helping you become "unstuck." 4-wheelin' is a hobby of mine and I've been "stuck" in my Jeep and in life more times than I care to admit, so I know the feeling well. It's not good at all.

So…my thoughts are that you're picking this book up because either curiosity is killing you or, you're stuck. You also could be using this as a resource for a class or lecture. Go, you! Regardless of the reason, I'm telling you that this book was written for those that are trapped and seeking a way out. Being stuck in the "mud of life" is no treat. It's like you get into a routine of doing things, following that same well known path, and before you know it, life goes on cruise control. Things may be fine for a while, heck, maybe even a few years. Eventually, something happens to you, or a friend, that makes you re-evaluate how you're doing things. Your buddy gets a huge promotion at work, your girlfriend just got engaged, or you start picking up that extra weight around the middle you strived so hard to keep off. After some self-reflection, you realize, "Crap, I'm in a rut!" Instantaneously, you begin to try and change things. You dust off your resume, commit to exercising daily, and begin to frequent new and different places. Some actions you commit to show promise; most don't, mainly due to lack of consistency.

The M.A.P. highlights major actions that individuals use to create positive change in their lives. This process was developed with input from clients, former students, their parents, and research from fourteen years in Education, four years in Mental Health Counseling/Behavior Therapy and seven years in Personal Development. The focus is on helping you develop a better life and ensure that you continue to grow on the path you desire.

Might I add that none of this is rocket science! This is a book anyone can pick up and start using. No advanced degrees needed, no piles of money to be spent...it's a simple plan that requests that you take it seriously, because it can produce serious results. I must also recommend that you read through this book a chapter per week. I chose a week because that will give you enough time to read through each chapter, digest it, select one or more activities to try, and obtain feedback or results before moving to the next section. After getting said feedback, modify the activity so it suits your life. Just because the book is final, doesn't mean that this is the final word. You should revise your life daily. Remember, this is a guide. Customize your world accordingly.

Included in each segment are the nuts and bolts strategies of how we will achieve your vision and goals. The chapter headings are the seven steps of The M.A.P. While reading, you will discover why each step is so critical to your success. There are suggestions that you can implement to expedite your journey through the book, but I leave it open for you to select them or choose an option of your own. Included are stories and examples that illustrate the concepts being taught, learning points and powerful questions that stir the mind to thought and eventual action. Probably my favorite parts of each chapter are the quotes scattered about. I love memorable statements from great thought leaders and honorable people. I believe that one's true wisdom can be summarized in twenty words or less. I promise you even implementing one of these strategies into your daily routine will positively impact the other areas of your well-being. Just make sure you're aware of the improvements...they will be subtle at first, but big changes always start small.

So, if you have conceded to defeat by stating "I'm stuck," just sit still and lemme throw you a tow rope. This book is your "tow rope." We're getting you out of the mud of life...you're welcome! I hope you enjoy reading it, but don't take too long though. This book is about taking MASSIVE ACTION...NOW! I'll see you in seven weeks!

Chester, GOODLIFE!! Coaching

"If you write your autobiography when you're old, you can see where you've been. If you write it when you're young, you can see where you're going!"

What Is Vison?

Vision is defined as "the act or power of anticipating that which will or may come to be." Every human being has vision, whether they know it or not. It is one of the spectacular things that make our species so great. At any given time that we want to change our destiny, with a little bit of determination and a whole lot of hard work, we can turn a vision into reality. The problem is that many of us choose to ignore our greater self because it seems too hard, or near impossible to attain, and the reality is that...yeah it is. But we have the ability to start the process towards making our thoughts manifest into being. Some believe in The Law of Attraction, which teaches that we are one with the Universe and everything is energy. We can create health and abundance simply by focusing our mind on it and "attracting" it to us via positive thoughts and energy. I've practiced it, and yes, even though it may seem like hocus pocus, your mind does actually bring it to you by allowing your eyes to "see" things and opportunities that once were invisible to you. The best example of this is how you begin to obsess over a new vehicle purchase, and all of a sudden that car is being driven by everyone. Actually, they've always been there...you just weren't focused on it. Now, you've drawn it to you. Although, having a vision goes deeper than that. Once you decide to go after your vision, the world...your world, begins to change, and any actions you make en route to your vision will lead to the next one until you have arrived at your destination. This is why having vision is so powerful. Think about it...businesses have visions for their products and services, pastors have visions for their ministry, and colleges and universities have visions for their students. Why shouldn't you have one for your life?

If your dreams don't scare you, they aren't
big enough. Lowell Lundstrum

Why Do I Need A Vision?

I believe it's very simple. Proverbs 29:18 says it best, "Where there is no vision, the people perish." It is critical that you have a vision because it is what will keep you going when things are moving in a positive direction, as well as when the world is crumbling down around you. People who have no vision will latch on to anything and everything, searching for themselves in the process. I say this for a few reasons, one of them being the multitude of people, particularly my young Black males, that cannot see themselves becoming anything successful other than a star athlete or musician. Now, I am by no means degrading the dedication of an athlete to their skillset, nor am I belittling a musician and their craft, but this special demographic need to see themselves in other lucratively successful careers. It serves as an alternative to when they don't make the team or don't land that gig. I can also liken this to the numerous fads and trends that are adopted, regardless of their negative origins or meanings. For example, the youth culture trend of "sagging" pants. Despite the very well-known history of this style (prison if you didn't know), our youth still wish to look like they have no access to a belt.

There are many potential leaders in this world that seek followers, but they too, may not have vision. You should be careful when choosing whom to follow in life. Those that lack direction, which is equally important, possibly lack the vision to lead as well.

Vision is the art of seeing the invisible. Jonathan Swift

How Do I Create My Vision?

Taking the necessary actions to begin building your vision is as simple as turning the television on, but instead of activating the remote, you activate your imagination. Here are some suggestions you can try to begin, starting with the easiest to the most involved.

Window Shop: Pick up a magazine catered toward the financially wealthy person called The DuPont Registry. It's a catalog for the rich to shop for boats, exotic cars, and elaborate homes. It sells for about $10...yes, it's pricey for a magazine, but can you put a price on your dreams? Anyway, if you don't want to spend the money on glossy sheets of paper (or you're an environmentalist) you can always click over to their website at www.dupontregistry.com and check out the offerings. Yes, it's shallow obsessing over goods as part of your vision, but I did say it was the easiest way to begin, right?

Dream Better Dreams: It is a proven fact that the last 10 minutes that you are awake is what your mind "chews" on while you are sleeping, and what you think about within the first 10 minutes of waking sets the tone for the rest of the day, but you didn't need research to know that, did you? We've all been there. You go to bed obsessing about something that bothered you that day and your mind revs over it all night. You wake up multiple times (other than to use the bathroom), and it keeps you from a sound night's sleep. Aren't you groggy and moody the next morning? Yep...not good. So to combat this, listen, watch, or read something positive, motivating, funny, and/or uplifting before going to bed at night (I personally like to watch Joel Osteen or The Fresh of Bel-Air reruns!). You can even talk to someone whom you know will lift you up. There is a reason that many people read a religious text just before bed and upon rising...it's not just for protection during our sleeping hours! Visit the site below for more information on dreaming better and having lucid dreams.   After reading the article and trying some of the techniques, I found it very helpful and have had some of the best and most vivid dreams ever. http://www.wikihow.com/Have-the-Dreams-You-Want.

<u>Take a Trip/Drive or go to an Open House:</u> Everyone knows that in order to gain a different perspective on life, you have to sometimes get into new environments, and we will talk more about that later. There is so much power in getting out and seeing the world, especially while on vacation. It allows the mind and body to unwind and re-vitalize. Many times, people have found a new appreciation for their lives back home after being away from it for an extended period of time. Take this time to really build your vision, as it may become more pronounced after some time off from work. Are you not prepared for a vacation yet? Take a drive through some local areas you've never been to and go see some of what I call "big houses." Although some luxury homes are inaccessible to outsiders (unless you live there or are invited in), some are easily driven past, but they're tucked away off the beaten path. Don't ask why...you already know the answer. Would you want people to know where you lived if they weren't invited? I didn't think so. Spend a day, or a weekend, "shopping" your local neighborhood for homes that you admire, or find an affluent neighborhood and drive through it. When you see the homes, start imagining your vehicle pulling up into one of the driveways. I've done it before with my wife...it's a great feeling, especially when you actually do pull up to one of those houses. It can happen! Better yet, an Open House allows you to dream build, and you can't be kicked

out if you're actually looking at the house. Have some questions for the realtor ready!

The Vision Board: You remember that $10 magazine I told you about? Yeah, that one! This is where you really get your money's worth out of the book. The Vision Board is where you take pictures of your perfect life from magazines and online printouts, cut them out, and stick them on a poster board. Then place it in a location where you will see it multiple times a day, every day. It's a fun project that anyone can do, and there is no wrong or right way to do it. It can have pictures, quotes, artwork, and it should have a picture of yourself somewhere on it, preferably during a time where you felt your best. You also don't have to use magazines or printed pictures. There's always the option of being really creative and drawing your vision board. That would make it extremely personal! My board has pictures of myself with my family all over and I like to place soul stirring fortune cookie messages on mine. I also have fitness goals, business goals, and a few material goals I want to attain. Which reminds me...don't make this completely materialistic. You may choose to (and should) include images that represent the healthy, emotional, spiritual, and family lifestyle that you desire as well.

Meet Your New Mentor (sort of): Read/research someone that is currently where you want to be. It could be a pastor, an athlete, a motivational speaker, teacher, politician, actor, musician, business person, or even a historical figure. It literally can be anyone. How did they arrive at their success? What trials and tribulations did they meet? You will realize that everyone has encountered hardships on their way to the top. Really internalize how they made their climb, and if you have to, make it your own blueprint to success.

The Vision Tape: A different take on the Vision Board but it serves the same purpose. What makes this incredibly difficult is that you have to have a vision of yourself already in your head, and you have to talk to yourself in the present from the future. I picked this strategy up during my training as a Coach, and I got so into it that I made 8 versions of myself from the future and added music to two of them! It was incredibly fun, but it took work to complete, mainly because of the recording. You don't have to be over the top with it like I was (heavy swagger, music in the background). Just record yourself, convincingly, that you are where you want to be 5 years from today.

One of my favorite artists to listen to and be inspired by is Katy Perry. Interesting enough that she too created a vision board, which was the catalyst for her stardom.

Katy Perry's Vision

Katy Perry made her first vision board in 1993, when Selena had won her first Grammy. Her teacher asked her class to create a vision board, and at 9 years old, she chose a picture of Selena with her Grammy. 15 years later, Perry was nominated for her first Grammy Award in the "Best Female Pop Vocal Performance" category, for her No. 1 Single "I Kissed A Girl," from her platinum Top 10 Album One of the Boys.[1]

If that wasn't good enough, how about one of Barack Obama's biggest supporters, Oprah Winfrey, using a vision board to help solidify the majority vote for him...at least in her eyes.

Oprah's Obama Vision

Talk show star Oprah Winfrey uses a vision board to visualize her goals and harness the power of intention. So what did Oprah have on her vision board? The gown she intended to wear to a very special event – the Obama inauguration.

Here's what Oprah told a New York radio station:

"I was speaking with Michelle and Caroline Kennedy and Maria Shriver – we were all doing a big rally out in California. At the end of the rally Michelle Obama said something powerful, 'and I want you to leave here and envision Barack Obama taking the oath of office.' I created a vision board. I had never had a vision board before. I came home, I got me a board and put Barack Obama's picture on it and I put a picture of my dress I want to wear to the inauguration."[3]

I guess the rest is history in both stories, huh? Good stuff, right? Yes, Vision Boards are a powerful foundation to get things going in the right direction. All you do is Seek, Cut, Paste, Apply!

Learning Points:

What are your Limiting Beliefs (things that you believe about yourself that may or may not be true, and prevent you from becoming who you were meant to be)?

There are one to two things in a person's life that are preventing them from being everything they can truly be.

Powerful Questions:

What do you value?

_____

_____

_____

_____

How would you describe yourself in a tweet?

_____

_____

_____

_____

Where do you see yourself in 1, 5, or 10 years?

_____

_____

_____

_____

If you could make a clone of a person you admire for today's world, who would it be and why?

_____

_____

_____

_____

Brief Assignment:

Pick one of the "How" activities from above and take your first action toward your better life. I must highly recommend The Vision Board and Tape. After all, the strategy is tried and true for me, friends I have, and many famous and successful people the world over. After you've completed your activity, talk to, contact your closest companion (preferably by voice or in person) and explain to them what you did and how it felt. Don't worry about their response; that will become important later on.

Write their name in the blank: _____

We will be coming back to their name in the future. Have Fun!

"I always knew I'd amount to something.
I guess I should have been more specific!"

What Are Goals?

A Goal by Google's definition is "the object of a person's ambition or effort; an aim or desired result." This is a great definition in my opinion because it speaks about two very important words, ambition and effort. When you ask someone if they have goals, everyone says yes. Now they may be unrealistic, some even unfiltered, but they are goals nonetheless. The issue with them is that sometimes said goals go unattained because of those words previously highlighted...many people lack ambition or don't want to put forth the effort to reach those goals which would ultimately make those visions a reality. The average person sets a goal and then expects to magically arrive at the destination, simply because it was conceived. Goals have to be acted upon at the moment of inception, or the momentum to follow through with the effort is lost. There is always something happening in life that can divert our attention from the goal causing derailment. Once derailment happens, the journey has to be started from the beginning, and why wouldn't it? We've lost the momentum we had, and now we have to get it back by working twice as hard.

So, we know that we all need to have goals, but the next level is to not limit ourselves with small goals, but to have incredible goals...GINORMOUS Goals! Darren Hardy, Publisher of SUCCESS Magazine calls them B.H.A.Gs (Big, Hairy, Audacious, Goals), but what does a Ginormous Goal look like? Well, I'm going to introduce another acronym here...S.M.A.R.T. (Specific, Measurable, Achievable, Realistic and Timely). This is where one looks at what it is they want to attain, whether it be material, emotional, or personal, and get very particular about what it is, what it looks like, and how long it will take them to achieve it. Ginormous Goals are also S.M.A.R.T. For example, someone may say "I want to be rich!" Well, that's a goal, but it's not Ginormous. A Ginormous Goal would look like this..."I would like to have a positive monthly balance of $500 in my checking account after all bills have been paid within the next 12 months." Okay, lets run the check...is it Specific? A positive balance after bills, Check! Is it Measurable? $500 per month within next 12 months, Check! Is it Achievable? Cut a corner here, create a side hustle, pack a lunch, brew coffee at home...yes it is! Check! Is it Realistic? $500 within a year, that gives 12 months to work on it, yes! Check! Lastly, is it Timely? Obviously, right? 12 months, Check! Now, we could break this down even further, but this is a great start. The beautiful thing about this goal is that even if they don't attain it, they will have seen progress towards it, and isn't that better than no progress at all? Isn't that the whole point...to move forward?

The trouble with not having a goal is that
you can spend your life running up and down the
field and never scoring. Bill Copeland

Why Do We Need Goals?

It's an interesting question for this step, because it's kind of pointless. "Why should someone have Goals?" Now, if a person asked 100 people this question, I'm sure they'd hear 100 different reasons, all with the same undertone. So let me be one of those 100 and say...how else could one expect to gain anything in life? Whether it's a new house, or a loving family, they have to have a goal that shows them when they've accomplished the objective. One would never know when to stop working hard, or take a break to enjoy what they've obtained if they had no goal. On that note, I will move to the next phase.

How Do I Create Goals?

Begin by doing the one thing that most people with goals fail to do...WRITE THEM DOWN! A composition book or journal works great, but any piece of paper will do, as long as it doesn't get lost! It may be easier to track if you tacked it somewhere close to your Vision Board, but like the board, you want to get in the habit of seeing it every day, so it too begins to adjust your actions daily.

Once you've found a method of writing them down, begin making broad goals, like "I want to lose weight." From there, start to hone the goal down to perfection, making them Ginormous and S.M.A.R.T. They should all resemble a format such as "I want to lose a total of 50 pounds within the next 5 months, by shedding no less than 2 pounds of fat per week." If you can make them more specific, then do so, but the worst thing you can do to hinder your progress is not to quantify or put a date on your success.

> *If you want to be happy, set a goal that*
> *commands your thoughts, liberates your*
> *energy, and inspires your hopes. Andrew Carnegie*

Les Brown is a motivational speaker and author, among many other things. His story is one of triumph over overwhelming odds, which has inspired millions to be their very best and obtain their goals and dreams. As you read below, think about a time where you had to "seize the moment" in order to reach your B.H.A.Gs.

The Les Brown Story

Les Brown and his twin brother were adopted by Mamie Brown, a kitchen worker and maid, shortly after their birth in a poverty-stricken Miami neighborhood. Because of his hyperactivity and nonstop jabber, Les was placed in special education classes for the learning disabled in grade school and throughout high school. Upon graduation, he became a city sanitation worker in Miami Beach. But he had a dream of being a disc jockey. At night he would take a transistor radio to bed where he listened to the local jive-talking deejays. He created an imaginary radio station in his tiny room with its torn vinyl flooring. A hairbrush served as his microphone as he practiced his patter, introducing records to his ghost listeners. His mother and brother could hear him through the thin walls and would shout at him to quit flapping his jaws and go to sleep. But Les didn't listen to them. He was wrapped up in his own world, living a dream. One day Les boldly went to the local radio station during his lunch break from mowing grass for the city. He got into the station manager's office and told him he wanted to be a disc jockey. The manager eyed this disheveled young man in overalls and a straw hat and inquired, "Do you have any background in broadcasting?" Les replied, "No sir, I don't." "Well, son, I'm afraid we don't have a job for you then." Les thanked him politely and left. The station manager assumed that he had seen the last of this young man. But he underestimated the depth of Les Brown's commitment to his goal. You see, Les had a higher purpose than simply wanting to be a disc jockey. He wanted to buy a nicer house for his adoptive mother, whom he loved deeply. The disc jockey job was merely a step toward his goal. Mamie Brown had taught Les to pursue his dreams, so he felt sure that he would get a job at that radio station in spite of what the station manager had said. And so Les returned to the station every day for a week, asking if there were any job openings. Finally the station manager gave in and took him on as an errand boy – at no pay. At first, he fetched coffee or picked up lunches and dinner for the deejays that could not leave the studio. Eventually his enthusiasm for their work won him the confidence of the disc jockeys that would send him in their Cadillacs to pick up visiting celebrities such as the Temptations and Diana Ross and the Supremes. Little did any of them know that young Les did not have a driver's license. Les did whatever was asked of him at the station – and more. While hanging out with the deejays, he taught himself their hand movements on the control panel. He stayed in the control rooms and soaked up whatever he could until they asked him to leave. Then, back in his bedroom at night, he practiced and prepared himself for the opportunity that he knew would present itself. One Saturday afternoon while Les was at the station, a deejay named Rock was drinking while on the air. Les was the only other person in the building, and he realized that Rock was drinking himself toward trouble. Les stayed close. He walked back and forth in front of the window in Rock's booth. As he prowled, he said to himself. "Drink, Rock, drink!" Les was hungry, and he was ready. He would have run down the street for more booze if Rock had asked. When the phone rang, Les pounced on it. It was the station manager, as he knew it would be.

"Les, this is Mr. Klein."

"Yes," said Les. "I know."

"Les, I don't think Rock can finish his program."

"Yes sir, I know."

"Would you call one of the other deejays to come in and take over?"

"Yes, sir. I sure will."

But when Les hung up the telephone, he said to himself, "Now, he must think I'm crazy." Les did dial the telephone, but it wasn't to call in another deejay. He called his mother first, and then his girlfriend. "You all go out on the front porch and turn up the radio because I'm about to come on the air!" he said. He waited about 15 minutes before he called the general manager.

"Mr. Klein, I can't find nobody," Les said.

Mr. Klein then asked, "Young man, do you know how to work the controls in the studio?"

"Yes sir," replied Les.

Les darted into the booth, gently moved Rock aside and sat down at the turntable. He was ready. And he was hungry. He flipped on the microphone switch and said, "Look out! This is me LB, Triple P – Les Brown, Your Platter Playing Poppa. There were none before me and there will be none after me. Therefore, that makes me the one and only. Young and single and love to mingle. Certified, bona-fide, indubitably qualified to bring you satisfaction, a whole lot of action. Look out, baby, I'm your lo-o-ove man." Because of his persistence and preparation, Les was ready. He wowed the audience and his general manager. From that fateful beginning, Les went on to a successful career in broadcasting, politics, public speaking and television.[4]

Entertaining story right? He tells it better than you reading it, but the story of Les motivates me every time I read it, and gets me pumped up when I hear it. The story illustrates how anyone with preparation, dedication, drive, and some patience, can realize their dreams, regardless of background and education. Some people may say that he was just "lucky." Les was in the right place at the right time. That may have been true, but had he not mentally prepared himself when the opportunity arose...had he not had a vision of becoming a DJ and a goal of purchasing a home for his mother, we may not have ever known about Les Brown – Motivational Speaker, and I can assure you we'd never even hear about Les Brown – City Groundskeeper. Anyone that has experienced any great success can tell you that it didn't just happen. It wasn't just "luck." They will instead paraphrase a great quote by a Roman philosopher named Seneca the Younger: "Luck is what happens when Preparation meets Opportunity."

A though before moving on...if you regret not acting on an opportunity or feel you were ill prepared for action, count it as the "fish that got away" and move on. There is no need dwelling on it, because when you do, you set yourself up to miss the next "big fish." Always be alert and prepared for the next opportunity that could lead you to your ultimate goals.

For myself, when opportunities are placed before me, I use an ultra-quick questioning strategy to determine if I need to act immediately, or give it more thought:

1. Could it help me?
2. Could it help my family?
3. Could it positively impact my goals?
4. Could it help me reach my goals quicker?

If my answer is yes to all of these questions, I think no more…I GO, MOVE, ACT…NOW! These opportunities only come around every few years for some people but lie around every corner for others. One opportunity usually leads to another, and another, until you have ultimately reached your goals. It's about aligning yourself with your surroundings and the people in it, expecting the opportunity to manifest, and being ready for it, like Les was.

Learning Points:

Your Goals are the fuel for your Vision. You only want the best fuel for your cars, and the best fuel for your body. You should only have the best fuel for your Vision as well.

Writing down your Goals is paramount to your success. Leave this step out and leave your Goals behind.

Your Goals should be S.M.A.R.T!

Powerful Questions:

What is a Small Goal for you? What is a Big Goal for you?
How can you make them "Ginormous?"

_____

_____

_____

_____

How will you track your progress?

_____

_____

_____

_____

Whom do you know that has set a goal and achieved it?
Have you spoken to them recently? What are they doing?

_____

_____

_____

_____

How would you celebrate attaining a Goal?

_____

_____

_____

_____

Brief Assignment:

<u>Write your Goals Down</u>: it's already been stated, but it warrants it again…writing your goals down is powerful. An old Chinese proverb says that "the faintest ink is more powerful than the strongest memory," meaning that it's hard to remember your goals when you've got millions of other thoughts going on inside your head at the same moment and it's better to write them down. Take a piece of paper and write down your Ginormous, S.M.A.R.T, B.H.A.G.s and place them where you will see them daily, and make many copies of it. Paste them on your Vision Board, in the Bathroom, in the car on your steering wheel, anywhere you spend vast amounts of time. To make it more special, place it in a beautiful notebook and dedicate a page to each goal. Write in the book with a special pen, and use it for that purpose only. At the top of each page, place the goal, and then section off the page for people that can help you attain it, how you plan to attain it, an end date, and even how you plan to celebrate when it's accomplished. How you organize your goals is up to you, just write them down!

"When opportunity knocked, I didn't recognize it.
It was disguised as hard work."

What Is Structure?

We all believe we don't need nor want it. The common statement is "I thrive in chaos," or "I work better under pressure." Although we deny structure, we begrudgingly need, desire, and even subconsciously demand it. Imagine walking into your new job ready to work, and a manager approaches you and tells you to work on whatever. You'd either have the most productive day ever or have earned the "Slacker of the Year" Award within two hours! Where is your workstation? How would you know what to do, who to report to, or even what time to wrap up for the day? Structure is important. Structure is the element for which our life is built upon. If someone lacks it, they tend to miss out on opportunities that will draw them closer to their Vision. Structure has another name that may be more familiar to us; especially our kids...Discipline...Self-Discipline to be exact. It is this and the creation of positive habits in our lives that allow us to reach our goals.

> *The time to repair the roof is when*
> *the sun is shining. John F. Kennedy*

Why Is Self-Discipline So Critical?

Self-Discipline is your backbone. There are distractions everywhere, and without discipline, derailment is inevitable. Think about this...let's say you get a response to a post on Facebook, Twitter, or Instagram. You pick up your smartphone, and look to see what was replied back to you. You smile, but then the mystical attraction to "scroll" takes over. You see a cute picture of your friend's toothless, grinning baby with ice cream up her nose. You "like" it, then you see a video clip of a cat dancing to Techno music, and you "like" that too. Then someone decides to debate with you about a tweet you posted, and you can't let that go without a rebuttal. Congratulations, you've officially become distracted, and without you knowing the tracks are running out right beneath you. Now for the next hour you will receive notifications about the link, post, pic, and response to everything you just activated. Goodbye productivity! It happens way too easily, and it's normal. There have been many studies conducted, especially with dogs and primates, that illustrate that we are conditioned to respond to the "bing." It alerts us to "someone that cares." Someone thought enough of what I said, posted, shared that they "liked" it. That must mean they like me. Not really, but people obsess over how many likes, follows, comments, tweets, hearts, shares, retweets one can acquire, and it gets distracting. The same can be said for phone calls, meal times, TV Shows, video games, emails...anything that prevents you from accomplishing a goal oriented task.

How Do I Become More Disciplined?

One of the easiest ways to create a self-disciplined mentality is creating Timers. Use a watch, smartphone, or even a regular egg timer will work...anything that allows you to countdown. Then decide what task is going to be done. Allot a specified time to complete the task or at least make major progress on it. Find a place of operation and do not allow any interruptions during that time. That means turning off or silencing anything that will "notify" you. Only stop for bathroom and water breaks. Give yourself time to get stuff done! Another strategy to use is to create Schedules for your day and week. It's amazing how infrequently we use the basic functions like the Calendar and Task List in our phones, and all phones have them. Block out time during the day to handle the most important things and let the lesser things fall to the Task List. A strategy I use is to place the things that need to be done daily on a sheet of paper and prioritize them in order from most important to the least. Section it off into 3rds, with the largest section at the top, the 2nd section medium width, and the 3rd section the thinnest. Place the most important tasks at the top, items of medium importance in the middle, and little importance at the bottom. Get the big stuff at the top out of the way and then check it off. The items that comprise the 3rd section...if you get to them, great. If not, place them at the top of the next day's list. But definitely try to get to the bottom! Give yourself a reward for finishing the list, so it makes getting things accomplished a pleasurable experience. Nothing too elaborate! Maybe a soda if you're on a diet, or an extra 15 minutes of TV time if you're working on curbing that behavior of excessive time in front of the tube. Committing to daily goals or to-do-lists will help create the discipline needed to reach your larger B.H.A.Gs.

We are what we repeatedly do, excellence then is not an act, but a habit. Aristotle

I came across this story when I did a Google search for "feats of great discipline." It didn't come up in the first few pages, as I was searching for something obscure to include in the book, and articles about The Mountain Man Dashrath Manji, fit the bill perfectly. If this doesn't illustrate a feat of great discipline, I challenge you to find a better example.

The Story of Dashrath Manjhi

Dashrath Manjhi, a landless farmer from India, made history after he spent over two decades chiseling away at a mountain with rudimentary tools, in order to create a road for his community, after the Government refused. Fifty-three years ago, he set out to carve a 1 km-long path through a rocky hillside, all by himself, in order to make it easier for his fellow villagers to access schools, markets and neighboring villagers. "This hill had given us trouble and grief for centuries. The people had asked the government many times to make a proper road through the hill, but nobody paid any attention. So I just decided I would do it all by myself," Manjhi told Indian newspaper Tehelka, in 2007, and shortly before succumbing to the cancer that was plaguing him. With just his chisel, hammer and shovel, this legendary man turned what was once a precarious one-foot-wide passage into a 360 ft-long, 30 ft-wide road accessible by bicycle and motorcycle.

The hill kept the region's villages in isolation, forcing people to trek through dangerous terrain for hours just to reach their lands or the nearest market town. Children had to walk eight kilometers to reach school, but thanks to Manjhi's handmade road, that distance has been reduced to three kilometers, and people from over 60 villages now use it every day.

But what empowered a single man to accomplish such a monumental task? For Dashrath it was the love for his wife. "My wife, Falguni Devi, was seriously injured while crossing the hill to bring me water; I worked then on a farm across the hills. That was the day I decided to carve out a proper road through this hill," the farmer said. Sadly, his beloved wife didn't get to see the fruits of his labor, as shortly after the accident she fell ill and died, because she couldn't be taken to the hospital in time. To reach the nearest hospital, he had to travel around the mountains, some 70 kilometers. The tragic loss only made the ambitious man more focused on his task, and fellow villagers remember seeing him "hacking at the hill day and night as if he were possessed." After plowing fields for others in the morning, he would work on his road all evening and throughout the night. He toiled from 1960 to 1982, having developed his own technique. He burned firewood on the rocks, and then sprinkled water on the heated surface which cracked the boulders making it possible to reduce them to rubble.

But with the passing years, his motivation changed. "My love for my wife was the initial spark that ignited in me the desire to carve out a road. But what kept me working without fear or worry all those years was the desire to see thousands of villagers crossing the hill with ease whenever they wanted," Manjhi said in an interview. Although you'd expect people to jump in and help someone working for the entire community, it wasn't Dashrath's case. He sold the family's three goats to buy the hammer and chisels and worked every day on the project to make it successful. At first, people ridiculed him and called him mad for taking on such a herculean task, but as time went by, and the unfazed farmer continued to split the troublesome hill in half, he started getting some help. "People told Manjhi that he wouldn't be able to do it," said Dahu Manjhi, the man's nephew, "that he is a poor man who just needs to earn and eat." Though most villagers taunted him at first, there were quite a few who lent support later by giving him food and helping him buy his tools. Now, all the people of the Gaya district have nothing but gratitude for the "mountain man" who single-handedly made their lives so much easier.

He received recognition from the Bihar government for his accomplishment in the form of a state burial, after he passed away, in 2007. The government also proposed his name for the Padma Shree award in 2006 in the social service sector. Nitish Kumar, the then Chief Minister of Bihar, proposed to build a 3 km metal clad road from Gehlour named after Manjhi and a hospital in his name in his village. "What I did is there for everyone to see. When God is with you, nothing can stop you," Dashrath once said. I am neither afraid of any punishment from any government department for my work nor am I interested in any honor from the government." It took him 22 years to fulfill his self-imposed task, but it granted him immortality. On his deathbed, Dathrash gave the okay for a film documentary to be done on his life. In 2012, Films Division has produced a documentary film on him "The man who moved the mountain" and the biopic movie *Manjhi – The Mountain Man* was recently completed in August 2015. According to the Indian Express, in the wake of the biopic, a special edition stamp will be issued in Manjhi's honor by the Bihar government.[6][8]

> *If you don't have a strong foundation*
> *the rest will crumble. Daymond John*

Learning Points:

What you do daily molds who you are and who you will become. Fill your days with positive habits.

A simple mind focused on a single purpose can surpass any great, unfocused mind.

Powerful Questions:

What habits do you have that could hinder your progress toward your goals and vision?

_____

_____

_____

_____

When do you find yourself the most undisciplined?

_____

_____

_____

_____

If you waiver, how will you "shock" yourself to get back on the right path?

_____

_____

_____

_____

Rule your mind or it will rule you. Horace

Brief Assignments:

<u>Create a Positive Habit and do it for 21 days.</u> Research has shown that it takes at least three weeks to make an action into a habit, and it takes longer for you to break it. The best way to do this is to track what you are doing and log it in a book/notebook every day that you do it. I have found in the past that whiteboard calendars work wonders, but any piece of poster board will do! When you "X" off every day that you complete it, and you see it daily, you'll not want to break the chain, therefore creating the discipline and creating the positive habit. And don't worry, if you mess up one day, just know that you have to make up that day at the end, and know that you may have lost some, if not all, momentum. Losing that may be even worse that missing the day.

<u>Create a Task List Template.</u> Also, make copies of it, so you never have to worry about drawing up another one daily. Just pull out a new one every day. Compile your list every morning when you wake up, or if you really want to get ahead, organize it the night before. There should be good ones to utilize as a basis or the program on MS Word under Templates.

For weight loss, <u>substitute one unhealthy food item for a healthier option.</u> Therefore, when self-discipline goes out the window, at least you'll have the healthy version of what you're "fiend"ing for.

For exercise, <u>track your activity by using a pedometer or smartwatch.</u> The more you move, the better you will feel, and yes housework counts as exercise. Most smart phones have accelerometers inside of them and track repetitious movement. Just download the app, input your settings, drop it in your pocket, and go.

"One man can change the world...
but you'll need a very big diaper!"

What does it mean to energize your environment?

Well, there is an ancient art form called Feng Shui practiced by the Chinese for over 4,000 years. It emphasizes how the environment one lives and the space they surround themselves in can dramatically influence their energy, health, wealth, happiness, and overall well-being. There must be something to it, because Feng Shui masters charge upwards of $1000 on the high end for client's homes to be "Shui"ed. Your environment is as critical to your vision and goals as cleanliness is to your health. Can you go without it, yes, but doing so will make it more difficult for success, and you'll stink to boot. You want your surroundings to be a reflection of who you want to be and where you want to go. Does it mean that you have to move from your neighborhood? At this time, no, but you may consider it in the future. The surroundings someone lives, works, and plays in says a lot about who they are and what they aspire to be. Your environment allows others to draw conclusions about you as well. People believe your actions and your environment more than what you say. Actions speak louder than words, and you can't inspire someone to be great when your life is in shambles.

There have been numerous studies about children, adults, animals, and even plant life that prove when a subject's environment is altered and improved, not only does their physical status improve, but their mental and emotional statuses improve as well.   Take for example your experience as a student in school.   Think back for a moment...who was that one teacher you would go out of your way to make and keep happy by having a great attitude, gifting, showing up early for class and staying late, studying for tests, participating during discussions, and always having your homework ready to turn in? Did you do that for all of your teachers, or just that one? Ask yourself why you strove so hard to make sure they stayed in good spirits? Did they have high expectations for every student? How about their classroom; was it bright, open, and cheerful?   Maybe they valued everyone's opinion. Here's a better question...are you always happy to talk to them, long after you've graduated? Let's be real...it was the environment you were in.   That teacher you remembered so well ensured that their class was one of positivity, positive energy, care, fun, interesting, and they ensured that you were going to enjoy school and be successful.   Everyone was expected to succeed.   Who wouldn't thrive in that environment?

> *What we see depends mainly on*
> *what we look for. John Lubbock*

Why Is Your Environment So Critical?

Most of us want to feel good, be happy, and live a long fruitful life. Your environment contributes to this and helps make that desire a reality. When your surroundings are in sync with the rest of your positive self (your vision, daily habits, etc.) it can literally make you feel like everything in your world is well. It's a great feeling...one that you try to keep clear of any negativity.

How Do You Begin Enhancing?

Start by getting rid of anything that makes you unhappy and replacing it with items that do. If there is a picture on your wall that makes you unhappy, replace it with something that inspires or motivates you. If you want to laugh more, watch a TV show or listen to radio that makes you laugh. If you find yourself feeling depressed, open a window and let some light inside. Remember that vision board we spoke about, make sure you put that up so you can see it...daily.

Change your thoughts and you
change the world. Norman Vincent Peale

A great example of how your environment can energize you is The City by the Bay: San Francisco. The City has made headlines as being one of the happiest, healthiest, and fittest cities in America, and was named the best city in America in 2012 by Bloomberg Businessweek. There are 12 reasons that give San Francisco its pizzazz, and reasons why your environment has a great deal in determining how fruitful you are in becoming "successful."

San Francisco: A Healthy Playground

The city is Veggie-Friendly, meaning that you will find an assortment of vegetarian and vegan menus and restaurants across the area, which is good, because a diet high in red meat can make you feel bad and cause damage to your body.

It has a vibrant spiritual life. Meditation, Yoga, and Eastern philosophy are part of what make the city. Any focus on spirituality is known to reduce stress and increase well-being. Yoga is everywhere, from public parks to the international airport, and is part of the New Age DNA of the city.

Its organic, the food I mean. There are farmers markets, community farms, organic restaurants, and food co-ops everywhere, and even though it directly doesn't affect your well-being as far as environment, ingesting the chemicals from commercial foods could put a damper on your health.

It is home to some of the best parks in the country. Walking through green spaces, even in the middle of cities, can put the brain into a state of meditation, according to research, and it has shown that public parks contribute to physical activity rates among city residents.

Outdoor activities are everywhere, from parks, to surfing, to public trails. There is something for everyone, and you don't even need a gym membership.

It's got loads of culture. There are outdoor theaters, live music, and literary events year round across the city, and studies have found that attending cultural events could lower blood pressure and also promote mental health by warding off anxiety and depression.

It's close to nature. Yeah we've already stated outdoors is good. We can all find ourselves by getting lost in nature.

It is one of the best cities for biking. The city even created 20 new miles of bike lanes, 25 bike parking areas, traffic signals for biker right of way and a $500 million hanging bike lane from the Bay Bridge. Research shows that biking and bike commuting can have a huge impact on health. One Danish study found that bikers had a lower risk of death from any cause than their more sedentary counterparts. And in a separate Australian study, researchers found that people who replaced their car commute with biking lowered their risk of stroke and heart attack, improved their cholesterol and their aerobic fitness within one year.

Locals drink wine in moderation for health benefits. Drink red wine and be healthy, for it lowers your risk of becoming overweight or obese. It contains heart healthy antioxidants and Resveratrol, which can reduce bad cholesterol.

It's a dog friendly city. Pets naturally help the body release endorphins, which in turn will reduce stress. They can improve heart health and help with mild depression.

It celebrates community with group volunteering activities and community art projects, which are linked to lower stress levels and increased will being and longevity. [2]

So, are you ready to move yet? Well, even if you aren't, incorporating some of the attributes of SF into your life will surely improve your environment.

Learning Points:

Even the smallest change in your environment can improve your well-being.

Some things in your environment that make you feel good now may bring you misery later. Keep the present and future in mind.

Your surroundings should reflect a better you, not where you currently are. This is where your Vision Board comes in handy!

Powerful Questions:

Are you happy with your surroundings? What will you do about it?

_____

_____

_____

_____

How is your environment a reflection of your personality/life?

_____

_____

_____

_____

What things need to happen, immediately and long term, in order to improve your surroundings?

_____

_____

_____

_____

Brief Assignment:

<u>Clean Up:</u> It's amazing how much a dirty room or cluttered environment can bring your mood down and rob your mojo. Do yourself a favor; if your home is due for a deep cleaning, make it happen this week. Take a room a day, and knock each one out until the house and yard are completely clean. The house will look brighter, smell better, be more inviting, and will boost your mood so you can power through your day. Not to mention you'll have a great place of reprieve at the end of a hectic one!   If you can, maybe even change some of the furniture around just for a different perspective.   Or if you're feeling really sprite, spruce up the interior with some paint.

<u>Explore Nature more (specifically somewhere with greenery and positive, flowing water):</u> We've said before, GET OUTSIDE! The color Green is the color of nature, fertility, and life. It symbolizes self-respect and well-being. If you feel a need for change, put Green in your life, and where else can you find it but outside in nature. Positive flowing water is water that is clean and refreshes. Think about how water meets an obstacle and flows around, under, or over it effortlessly. It's a metaphor for a good life...when you run into an obstacle, simply move on. Water that can't flow becomes stagnant, dirty, and smelly. Although life can exist and bloom in this environment, it's probably not the life you're seeking (think mosquitoes!).

Eat at a different restaurant than you normally do (preferably non-American): Not only will you get around a different group of people and in a new environment, which in itself can inspire creativity, but you'll also get to experience a new tasty dish. You remember those pleasure endorphins, right?

Purchase some Lucky Bamboo, or Lavender: Plant life is the best way to bring the outdoors inside, along with the color Green. Lucky Bamboo is a beautiful plant often confused with actual Bamboo, which grows in the wild and has roots that run deep. Lucky Bamboo is perfect as a house plant, as its leaves and roots only grow so long. It's very easy to maintain, and is a very hardy plant. When purchasing Bamboo, they can come in many different arrangements and quantity, which all mean various things. No matter what, never accept or purchase a plant with four stalks. The number four sounds like the word for "death" in Chinese and the number also carries negative connotations and energy. Lavender is a plant known for its calming properties. Its scent has been proven by research to do so. Placing the leaves in a vase beside your bed or heating lavender oil in an oil burner will help you relax and fall asleep faster, along with using other sleep aids like silencing your electronics, avoiding caffeine before bed, and room temperature control.

<u>Buy a pet:</u> Pets are known to help reduce stress as we've already said, but it's not just from their mood altering antics like getting caught in a paper bag, or howling with us while we sing in the shower, but they get us up and moving, and that alone alters your positive well-being. Every morning and every night, Fido has to be walked. Every day Nibbles' cage needs to be cleaned, and daily we are shooing animals off of furniture. Pets also calm us by being your furry, feathered, or finned friend that you can talk to, snuggle with, and keep you company when you're feeling alone. The best thing about pets...they don't judge you, and don't we all want that? A pet is possibly the only living thing that will cherish you for who you are flaws and all. Plus, you're their meal ticket, so they kind of have to! I have two cats named Busy and Wi-Fi (read: my son and wife have two cats). They bug me incessantly with their constant ankle grazing and make it incredibly difficult to walk from the kitchen to the living room, but they're also great for a chuckle, especially when they race! I've seen more cats crash into walls than I ever needed to see.

"Why do I need to learn potty training? Is it something I'll use later in life? Will it help me get into a good college? Do chicks dig guys who are potty trained?"

What Is A Support Team?

We all know these sayings and how they go..."Birds of a feather flock together," or "Tell me who you're friends are and I'll tell you who you are," and the favorite, "If all your friends jumped off a bridge, would you do it?" The truth is, probably so! When we spoke about environment in the previous step, that included the people in your life as well, but it's such an important element that it deserved its own section.

The people you surround yourself with are incredibly essential to your success personally and professionally. They are so important that books have been written, sermons and presentations have been given, school philosophies are built upon it, and court cases have been decided based on it. Your "entourage," "croonies," "familia," a.k.a. friends can launch you into better circumstances and situations, or they can bring you down in to the doldrums of nothingness. Misery loves company, but so does prosperity. The issue is that prosperity requires effort, misery does not.

Have you ever met someone that seems like they just have everything together? Everyone likes them. Everyone wants to be in their presence, and they're invited to all the elite events, where the who's who of the area will also be in attendance. Those individuals are usually very careful about who they let into their circle. Oh sure, they may seem warm, inviting, and friendly, but they have ways of identifying if you would be one of the people that they'd want to be affiliated with. You see, these successfully popular people have a great deal to lose in their personal and professional lives when it comes to their affiliations. Yes, you want to be with someone that can ebb and flow with every type of personality out there, but every person can't handle the environments. It makes them uncomfortable. So, they seek out other people that mirror themselves. But, if you are trying to become prosperous, why would you involve yourself with someone that has less than you spiritually, emotionally, financially, and the like, unless you were helping them evolve into a better version of themselves? Why would you involve yourself with someone that is not going to support you and your dreams, goals, and aspirations? We were all meant to live an abundant life, so why shouldn't we want to meet others that are also in that quest? You want people around you to cheer you on, pick you up when you get knocked down, wipe your brow, and then throw you back in the ring, not drag you out of the ring and then sit on the sideline with you, upset that you lost. Gary Vaynerchuk recently stated in an interview on the #AskGaryVee Show (Episode 118) that his number of people to surround himself with is 10...5 people that inspire you, you want to be around, and level you up, and 5 more people that you inspire and are helping move to the next level. Sound advice! Give back and you shall receive.

People that may be whispering sweet negatives into your soul don't have to be in person either. You could be receiving these messages from the TV shows you watch (JERRY! JERRY!), the news you read, and the music you listen to. Be conscious of your media choices. Only foster your positive thinking with voices that educate, explain, or energize you. This includes your own voice. My personal recommendation of choice would be listening to Dr. Eric "E.T." Thomas the Hip-Hop Preacher. His story, energy, and method of delivering his messages are truly amazing and inspiring.   Catch him on his site at www.etinspires.com. Don't forget, you can always inspire yourself from the future by using your freshly minted Vision Tapes as well!

It takes a great deal of bravery to stand
up to our enemies, but just as much to stand
up to our friends. J.K. Rowling

Why Do I Need One?

We want people around us that are going to show us the way and possibly help us get there. I've had the fortunate opportunity to marry a woman that loves to give back through her employment, as well as volunteering with Habitat for Humanity. The people I have met through her, both with extensive financial means and those without, have shown me that there are good people still in this world, and they want to help other good people. The individuals at Habitat really want to help families secure "the American Dream" of owning a home, and those that get selected for those homes have been thoroughly screened to make sure that they will assist the organization in furthering their efforts to put more people in their homes. "Iron Sharpens Iron" (Proverbs 27:17) has been the premise of good people helping other good people. Prosperous, generous, and forward thinking individuals normally interact with others of the same caliber. Volunteering your talents and time is one thing. Being formally requested to join their ranks though not only could be seen as an honor, but a welcome to share your thoughts, ideas, and energy with the group. My wife began as a volunteer, giving back because her work could positively influence the Habitat process. Now she is sought after by multiple groups on a regular basis.

How Do I Create A Support Team?

The process is simple...get away from people that pull you down, and get around people that will pull you up. This can happen by traveling to new places, or at its core, introducing yourself to someone new that you recently met. Don't be afraid to open your mouth and say "Hi!" Many people feel that it's hard or too intimidating to introduce yourself to new people. To ease the pain or displeasure of doing so, make conversation at or about events that you are familiar with. Common grounds to always talk up new people have always been Family and

Activities. The Order of Man Periscope/Podcast took it a step further with the acronym F.R.O.G. (Family, Recreation, Occupation, Goals). They are fairly neutral topics that everyone likes to talk about, especially when it's about them. Stay away from subjects you don't know about, really have no interest in, or don't fit the environment you are currently in. For example, if you don't know about sports or video games, don't talk up someone about it, because you don't know how deep the other person's knowledge is about it. It may be deeper than yours, which could paint you into a corner conversationally and end the encounter quicker than it started. Also when having conversations, don't talk about the weather; it shows that you have no conversation skills or creativity. Lastly, stay away from highly contested topics such as politics, economics, and religion unless you are VERY versed in the topics and are willing to "battle" verbally in public. Try to keep conversations light hearted. Sometimes, all it takes to make a new acquaintance is asking the right questions and simply listening. You could also use a Wingman...just a thought!

You're going to come across people in your life who will say all the right words at all the right times. But in the end, it's always their actions you should judge them by. It's actions, not words, that matter. Nicholas Sparks

A couple of things to think about before venturing off to find your new group of acquaintances, associates, and friends...

Be Deliberate about your Decision. You can't decide to get around new people and then let it flounder. Be deliberate about it. Make a plan to meet new people, carry it out, and then make it a habit.

Be Willing to Shed the Dead Weight. Sometimes, the people that you feel are supporting you are holding you back. They may have served their purpose in getting and keeping you where you are today, but in order to reach a new level, you have to be willing to let go of those that don't want to move with you.

Try New Things. Okay, I get it. You're in a comfortable place with yourself, and that's okay. Just realize that those new people you are looking for are out doing things that you may have never done before. Don't be afraid to try something new, even if it doesn't fall on your radar as "something you normally would do," because that's the whole point. When you do something that you normally wouldn't, it creates access to places where you meet new and interesting people. Get out of your comfort zone!

Seek Out Those Communities. We will talk some about "meetups" further down, but when you try new things, you get tied into new communities if you choose to become a regular. The best way to meet new people in their environment is to become a Chameleon. Go to a community and mingle with the regulars. Make it a point to go to different places and interact. Become an active participant in your socialization. You don't have to be the life of the party, but the party can breathe new life into you.

Go Online! It is easier than ever now to get and stay connected. With computers, tablets, smartphones, and the like, you can find anything, anyone, any hobby or interest and the communities they reside in online. From guys that drink a specialty beer per week and review it to women that knit coats for cats, you can find your place via the Web. Not to mention most communities online are fun, interactive, engaging, very open to newbies, and meet occasionally in person. So don't be afraid to check out your wildest, most creative, weirdest interests…I'm sure there's a community online for it.

Below are two versions of a story about an Eagle who believed it was a Chicken. They both begin very similar, but they end very differently. What makes them different is the person that breathes life or death into them. The Farmer and Ecologist play a critical part in the success of the Eagle. If you were the Eagle (and you are!), who would be the people that influence your flight?

The Eagle Who Thought He Was a Chicken

A baby eagle became orphaned when something happened to his parents. He glided down to the ground from his nest but was not yet able to fly. A man picked him up. The man took him to a farmer and said, "This is a special kind of barnyard chicken that will grow up big." The farmer said, "Don't look like no barnyard chicken to me." "Oh yes, it is. You will be glad to own it." The farmer took the baby eagle and placed it with his chickens.

The baby eagle learned to imitate the chickens. He could scratch the ground for grubs and worms too. He grew up thinking he was a chicken.

Then one day an eagle flew over the barnyard. The eagle looked up and wondered, "What kind of animal is that? How graceful, powerful, and free it is." Then he asked another chicken, "What is that?" The chicken replied, "Oh that, it's an eagle. But don't worry yourself about it. You will never be able to fly like him."

And the eagle went back to scratching the ground. He continued to behave like the chicken he thought he was. Finally he died, never knowing the grand life that could have been his. [5]

That wasn't even a horror story and it scared me! Here's the next one, which has a little more "meat" to it.

The Fable of the Eagle and the Chicken

A fable is told about an eagle who thought he was a chicken. When the eagle was very small, he fell from the safety of his nest. A chicken farmer found the eagle, brought him to the farm, and raised him in a chicken coop among his many chickens. The eagle grew up doing what chickens do, living like a chicken, and believing he was a chicken.

An ecologist came to the chicken farm to see if what he had heard about an eagle acting like a chicken was really true. He knew that the eagle-was king of the sky. He was surprised to see the eagle strutting around the chicken coop, pecking at the ground, and acting very much like a chicken. The farmer explained to the ecologist that this bird was no longer an eagle. He was now a chicken because he had been trained to be a chicken and he believed that he was a chicken.

The ecologist knew there was more to this great bird than his actions showed as he "pretended" to be a chicken. He was born an eagle and had the heart of an eagle, and nothing could change that. The man lifted the eagle onto the fence surrounding the chicken coop and said, "Eagle, thou art an eagle. Stretch forth thy wings and fly." The eagle moved slightly, only to look at the man; then he glanced down at his home among the chickens in the chicken coop where he was comfortable. He jumped off the fence and continued doing what chickens do. The farmer was satisfied. "I told you it was a chicken," he said.

The ecologist returned the next day and tried again to convince the farmer and the eagle that the eagle was born for something greater. He took the eagle to the top of the farmhouse and spoke to him: "Eagle, thou art an eagle. Thou dost belong to the sky and not to the earth. Stretch forth thy wings and fly." The large bird looked at the man, then again down into the chicken coop. He jumped from the man's arm onto the roof of the farmhouse.

Knowing what eagles are really about, the ecologist asked the farmer to let him try one more time. He would return the next day and prove that this bird was an eagle. The farmer, convinced otherwise, said, "It is a chicken."

The ecologist returned the next morning to the chicken farm and took the eagle and the farmer some distance away to the foot of a high mountain. They could not see the farm nor the chicken coop from this new setting. The man held the eagle on his arm and pointed high into the sky where the bright sun was beckoning above. He spoke: "Eagle, thou art an eagle! Thou dost belong to the sky and not to the earth. Stretch forth thy wings and fly." This time the eagle stared skyward into the bright sun, straightened his large body, and stretched his massive wings. His wings moved, slowly at first, then surely and powerfully. With the mighty screech of an eagle, he flew. [5]

I have always enjoyed reading this fable. It puts so much in perspective: your environment, the people you surround yourself with, being fearful vs. taking a chance...it's all there! Did you see how easy it was for the Eagle to just accept his fate as a Chicken, based on what the Farmer and other chicken told him? Who in your life has behaved in this manner? Do you still talk to them? Are you still friends with them? If so, ask yourself if you could do better than that relationship. On the other hand, did you see how the Ecologist refused to acknowledge the grim fate of the Eagle, and persisted with strategy after strategy until he was successful? Is there anyone in your life like this? Who refuses to give up on you? How would it feel to have an entire support squad of "Ecologists?"

If one is desperate for love, I suggest looking at one's friends and family and see if love is all around. If not, get a new set of friends, a new family. Jasmine Guy

Learning Points:

Sometimes the people you hold dear are also the people who are holding you back.

Your inner circle is a direct reflection of your personality, morals, values, and beliefs.

You want people in your environment to boost you up, not pull you down.

Surround yourself with people who make you happy. People who make you laugh, who help you when you're in need. People who genuinely care. They are the ones worth keeping in your life. Everyone else is just passing through.
Karl Marx

Powerful Questions:

If you and (insert positive, influential person, alive or deceased) became new friends, which of your current friends would you introduce to them first? Why?

_____

_____

_____

_____

What qualities do you like about yourself?

_____

_____

_____

_____

When was the last time you were "boosted up" by one of your friends? What was the setback you had to overcome?

_____

_____

_____

_____

Brief Assignment:

<u>Join a Meetup Group and go "meetup."</u> Meetup.com is a website that allows users to find local groups that have the same interests as you. Meet them at their next engagement. Meetups can range from topics about business and family, to music and video games, plus everything in between. Whether you know it or not, there's usually a meetup group located within 25-30 minutes of your address, and they usually meet weekly, bi-weekly, or at the least monthly. These functions get you involved with a new group of people and offer networking opportunities.

<u>Find a Social Game/App like Ingress.</u> Ingress is a Social Augmented Reality game played with Apple and Android devices across digital cell signals and/or Wi-Fi. Although the point of the game is like a real world "Capture the Flag" game, the best part about it is the social interactivity. They have local, district, state, regional, and even national groups that are always playing and looking to meet new teammates. Anomalies are huge gatherings of players in major cities where objectives at certain "portals" must be achieved, and First Saturdays are cross-faction gatherings of veteran and newbie players that meet up to help the new guys learn the game. Ingress participants are friendly and always willing to lend a helping hand in the quest for "world domination" for their faction. The only barrier to participation is whether you have an Apple or Android

smartphone or not...and who doesn't have one of those right now? (Sorry Windows and Blackberry!) But there are a multitude of apps just like this; from zapping aliens to fitness quests, I'm sure you will find one that suits you. Then go play! If you download Ingress and join The Enlightenment (The Green Team), tweet me a screenshot of your screen name during Levels 1-3 @AG00DLIFE and I will personally send you a Limited Edition Green GOODLIFE Double Eye Smartphone Cleaning Sticker FREE!

<u>Join a local non-profit organization or volunteer.</u> Like I stated previously with my wife and Habitat, not only will you be helping another person in need, it feels incredible knowing that what you are doing to help another human being (or animal) makes them feel so empowered. Helping really is addictive, so be sure not to spread yourself too thin doing so. Commit to one organization or cause. Then if you feel you can handle another, add another. Most importantly, make sure you can "show up." No cause needs another volunteer that doesn't participate. Step in and step up. Also, if you feel that what the organization is doing is not benefiting the cause, speak up. People will see that you are genuinely invested in the group, and will look to you for leadership, guidance, and decision making. All of this brings you around a new, more diverse group of people.

<u>Strike up a conversation with a complete stranger.</u> It literally can be ANYONE and ANYWHERE. Just try it out. You see someone standing in line behind you, talk about their shoes...even if you don't like them, and compliment them! It works better if you are authentic, so seek something out that you'd like to talk to them about. At the gas station and you see a nice car, compliment them on it. Ask questions about them. "I like your hair; where'd you get it cut?" I personally like to check out people's watches and men's ties, because I'm a watch and tie guy. Keep your eyes open for opportunities to speak to people. Everyone's favorite topics to talk about are themselves, their family, and their belongings. Open the doors to allow them to do so.

<u>Change the Channel (TV and/or Radio).</u> Every so often your TV resets during an electrical storm or when you pull the cables off your car battery the radio memory resets. This is a good thing, because sometimes you end up on a channel that you normally wouldn't have tuned in to. Change is good, and necessary to gain a greater perspective on life and career. I was never a fan of NPR radio, but my wife loves it. When I happened to drive her vehicle one morning, there was a very interesting interview about the recent Disney Pixar movie *Inside Out* and how the movie is being used by psychologists and counselors to illustrate to kids their emotions, how it's okay to be sad, and how emotions can be confusing, all in a visual, humorous way.

Had that station not been on, I wouldn't have been exposed to this new tool being used for child study. By the way, it was a GREAT movie (my subtle endorsement)!

"Remember son, when life hands you lemons, try, try again because a penny saved gathers no moss. That pretty much covers everything."

What About My Journey?

At this time you have learned and committed to everything that one needs to begin working on the rest of their life. In the beginning, you were simply being introduced and practicing everything in this book. From framing your vision to surrounding yourself with the essential people that will move you forward, everything you have done up to this point has been rehearsal, even though you have made great strides in your advancement. It is at this time that you begin to utilize all of your teachings and start modifying them to work better for your personality, personal, and professional situations.

The journey of a thousand miles
begins with the first step. Lao Tzu

Why Do I Need To Take This Journey?

Well, this is the fledgling being pushed from the nest. You will either fly or fall. We all want to and hope to fly when the time is right for us to do so, but falling isn't necessarily a bad thing either. It's only bad or harmful if you decide to stay on the ground with the wolves opposed to getting up and trying to fly again, or trying with a new strategy. Penguins are birds and they can't fly from predators, but boy can they slide on their bellies!

How Should I Make It?

Don't delay! Take everything you've learned and go out into the world! Begin LIVING the life you deserve, and of the most importance...PRACTICE what you've learned! Be conscious of your environment. Be aware of your inner circle, and be alert to your thoughts and emotions. Don't live your life on cruise control, because the car driving on its own does not take into account the beauty and intricacies of the journey! The photo opportunities on Route 66, the big Sombrero Tower at South of the Border, or just driving Skyline Drive are all part of the journey toward your ultimate destination. Life is meant to be lived. YOU drive the vehicle!

> *You must be fearless to travel on the
> journey of unknown. Lailah Gifty Akita*

The legend of The Phoenix is one of a great journey about transformation. Anyone that knows about Phoenixes, whether from stories or the character Dumbledore from Harry Potter, knows that the bird dies and is reborn from its ashes. The old self is laid to rest and the new, better, enlightened self emerges. It is an awesome metaphor for great changes in one's life and journeys that transform and evolve the traveler.

The Phoenix

There is a bird that lays no eggs and has no young. It was here when the world began and is still living today, in a hidden, faraway desert spot. It is the Phoenix, the bird of fire.

One day in the beginning times, the sun looked down and saw a large bird with shimmering feathers. They were red and gold; bright and dazzling like the sun itself. The sun called out, "Glorious Phoenix, you shall be my bird and live forever!"

Live forever! The Phoenix was overjoyed to hear these words. It lifted its head and sang, "Sun glorious sun, I shall sing my songs for you alone!"

But the Phoenix was not happy for long. Poor bird, its feathers were far too beautiful. Men, women, and children were always casing it and trying to trap it. They wanted to have some of those beautiful, shiny feathers for themselves.

"I cannot live here," thought the Phoenix and it flew off toward the east, where the sun rises in the morning.

The Phoenix flew for a long time, and then came to a far away, hidden desert where no humans lived. And there the Phoenix remained in peace, flying freely and singing its songs of praise to the sun above.

Almost five hundred years passed. The Phoenix was still alive, but it had grown old. It was often tired, and it had lost much of its strength. It couldn't soar so high in the sky, nor fly as fast or as far as it was young.

"I don't want to live like this," thought the Phoenix. "I want to be young and strong."

So the Phoenix lifted its head and sang, "Sun, glorious sun, make me young and strong again!" but the sun didn't answer. Day after day the Phoenix sang. When the sun still didn't answer, the Phoenix decided to return to the place where it had lived in the beginning and ask the sun one more time.

It flew across the desert, over hills, green valleys, and high mountains. The journey was long, and because the Phoenix was old and weak, it had to rest along the way. Now, the Phoenix has a keen sense of smell and is particularly fond of herbs and spices. So each time it landed, it collected pieces of cinnamon bark and all kinds of fragrant leaves. It tucked some in among its feathers and carried the rest in its claws.

When at last the bird came to the place that had once been its home, it landed on a tall palm tree growing high on a mountainside. Right at the top of the tree, the Phoenix built a nest with the cinnamon bark and lined it with the fragrant leaves. Then the Phoenix flew off and collected some sharp-scented gum called myrrh, which it had seen oozing out of a nearby tree. The Phoenix made an egg from the myrrh and carried the egg back to the nest.

Now everything was ready. The Phoenix sat down in its nest, lifted its head, and sang, "Sun, glorious sun, make me young and strong again!"

This time the sun heard the song. Swiftly it chased the clouds from the sky and stilled the winds and shone down on the mountainside with all its power.

The animals, the snakes, the lizards, and every other bird hid from the sun's fierce rays, in caves and holes and under shady rocks and trees. Only the Phoenix sat upon its nest and let the sun's rays beat down upon it's beautiful, shiny feathers.

Suddenly there was a flash of light, flames leaped out of the nest, and the Phoenix became a big round blaze of fire.

After a while the flames died down. The tree was not burnt, nor was the nest. But the Phoenix was gone. In the nest was a heap of silvery-gray ash.

The ash began to tremble and slowly heave itself upward. From under the ash there rose up a young Phoenix. It was small and looked sort of crumpled, but it stretched its neck and lifted its wings and flapped them. Moment by moment it grew, until it was the same size as the old Phoenix. It looked around, found the egg made of myrrh, and hollowed it out. Then it placed the ashes inside and finally closed up the egg. The young Phoenix lifted its head and sang, "Sun, glorious sun, I shall sing my songs for you alone! Forever and ever!"

When the song ended, the wind began to blow, the clouds came scudding across the sky, and the other living creatures crept out of their hiding places.

Then the Phoenix, with the egg in its claws, flew up and away. At the same time, a cloud of birds of all shapes and sizes rose up from the earth and flew behind the Phoenix, singing together, "You are the greatest of birds! You are our king!"

The birds flew with the Phoenix to the temple of the sun that the Egyptians had built at Heliopolis, city of the sun. Then the Phoenix placed the egg with the ashes inside on the sun's altar.

"Now," said the Phoenix, "I must fly on alone." And while the other birds watched, it flew off toward the faraway desert.

The Phoenix lives there still. But every five hundred years, when it begins to feel weak and old, it flies west to the same mountain. There it builds a fragrant nest on top of a palm tree, and there the sun once again burns it to ashes.

But each time, the Phoenix rises up from those ashes, fresh and new and young again. [7]

How awesome is that? This story is about reinvention, regeneration, jump starting one's life when you feel stagnant. Think about times when you have started a new job, a new workout routine, a new endeavor. You get revitalized and everything starts looking up for you. Just remember when the journey gets long, find a way to revitalize yourself periodically so you never lose momentum. Consistency is the key to success.

No one is going to hand me success. I must go out & get it myself. That's why I'm here. To dominate. To conquer. Both the world, and myself. Unknown

Learning Points:

Humans are the most unique species on Earth, unlike any other. At any given time we can alter our future by changing our mindset. No other creature can do this; their DNA has preprogrammed them to do what they do as animals, which makes us the most superior. In that same vein, you are the only person that can change your mindset, and no one else, which also makes you the most superior over your life.

Powerful Questions:

Why do you want to be a better you?

_____

_____

_____

_____

When during the reading of this book did you know that you were committed to the change?   What was the catalyst?

_____

_____

_____

_____

Where do you feel this journey will take you?

_____

_____

_____

_____

Are you ready for it and willing to sacrifice what needs to be let go in order to reach your higher self? What other tools do you need to make this journey?

_____

_____

_____

_____

Chronicle your journey...begin writing daily in a journal. Write whatever comes to your mind...draw it if you have to. Just be sure to write every day. You can, and should, write multiple times if you desire. You want to be able to reflect back on the journey once you have arrived at your destination.

Interlude

STOP!! Before You Go Any Further…

It is at this time that I must ask that you stop reading this book and re-evaluate if you have done everything that has been listed in this program. Before you move to the last chapter, have you really done EVERYTHING?

I ask this because in the process of writing this book, editing it, proofing it, rewriting it, and working with a host of clients, I have seen great growth in myself and people I have coached. Although, the results have been phenomenal, I have also seen participants go through this book and completely negate everything stated in each chapter, and their lives have not gotten any better than when they initially picked up the book.

I will make this claim…the material you have previously read WORKS, but it only works if YOU WORK! That has been the key element to everyone's success that has read this text. When they work on themselves, they improve every facet of their lives. It is impossible for it not to work, if you are consciously applying everything asked of you.

So, before turning the page, would you please help me help you? If you haven't cleaned your house, clean it. If you are still spewing negative comments about people, stop it. If you haven't sought out a new interesting group of people to interact with, seek them out. TAKE ACTION!

This is The M.A.P...The MASSIVE ACTION PLAN! You MUST take MASSIVE ACTION NOW in order to see your life change!

Thank You and know that I Love You! Turn the page and I'll see you on the other side.

Chester, GOODLIFE!! Coaching

Step 7: You Have Arrived!!

"I'm finally successful enough to use a really expensive pen — and I want to make sure people notice!"

What's Goin' On?

Success! You have become the person you have always wanted to be! Congratulations! For those that need the extra moments, no problem! Yours will come in due time. It will still be here for you. That is the beautiful thing about personal development...it's personal. Your pace, your time, your goals, your decisions. It's time for you to enjoy the bounty from your harvest. You've earned it! Quick questions...did you turn the page right after you read it? Were you ready for it, or did you go back and reevaluate? Did you take some time...a day, a week, a month? Regardless of the time, it doesn't matter. You're here! Are you ready for the next part? I hope so, because although you have arrived, the journey is far from over.

Accept responsibility for your life. Know that it is you who will get you where you want to go, no one else.
Les Brown

Why Is It Such A Big Deal?

You see, what you have accomplished was a great feat. Some people will never realize how great they can be. This was a personal journey though, and the greatest joy and success comes from building something greater than us, fulfilling a cause greater than us. It is our responsibility as people to give back from whence we came. Think of yourself like a tree...you grow daily, and when you are able to share your seeds of knowledge, inspiration, and economic ability with others, you are returning back to Earth what you borrowed from it, similar to how someone in your past seeded you with their knowledge. It means nothing to keep it all for yourself, because when your time here in this life is over, you exit only with what you entered in with. Those that supported you then probably want nothing from you now other than to see you successful, so instead of returning the acts of kindness, you pay it forward, and help someone else.

Where Do I Go From Here?

Create a new cause, donate from the heart, share with the world all of your being.

There are many stories about great individuals that gave of themselves once they believed they had arrived. Rev. Dr. Martin Luther King believed he had arrived, and began speaking out for the civil rights of Blacks. Sir Richard Branson, an entrepreneur very early on, believed he had arrived and began funding some of the largest philanthropic initiatives in the world, including The Elders, The Carbon War Room, and The International Centre for Missing & Exploited Children. Nelson Mandela fought against apartheid in Africa. Bill Gates has created The Bill & Melinda Gates Foundation for Education. Oprah Winfrey created Oprah's Angel Network. Warren Buffet of Berkshire Hathaway donates to Healthcare, extreme poverty, education, access to information technology, and the list could go on. These were all people that once they had risen to the top of their mountain, they looked over at the larger, more profound mountain in the distance and began the journey to climb that one.

The best revenge is MASSIVE success! Frank Sinatra

Learning Points:

The process is short, but the road is long, and sometimes even lonely. It's better if you take someone with you.

You are not alone in your greatness on this planet. The world needs your light to shine brighter.

Powerful Questions:

Are your reasons for starting this journey the same as when you finished? What changed? What stayed the same? Why?

_____

_____

_____

_____

How will you "reseed" the soil that you grew from?

_____

_____

_____

_____

Your Final Assignment

Teach and share with someone that you believe would benefit from your mentoring so they too can be inspired to become their better self. Choose them carefully, because those that are in need of your time, talents, and dedication aren't necessarily those that deserve your resources. I've had to learn this the hard way in the past, and I still misjudge occasionally. Always remember to keep your cup full, so the overflow will fill others. When you take time to do this (through regular exercise, volunteering, eating right, and feeding your mind with positive messages), it will not matter if you are pouring into those that are deserving of you or not...your cup is already filled.

Though no one can go back and make a brand new start, anyone can start from now and make a brand new ending.
Carl Bard

The book you have just read is a manual to a better life. With this, you will be able to help others who may need your assistance in order to see the light in themselves, and it will always be there if you need a "refresher."

I would like to once again thank you for your time in reading my work. It has been a great ride, and I'll see you in your new life!

Acknowledgements

At this time I would like to acknowledge the people that have made this publication possible.

First up is my editor, Lakishia Bannister. After writing this book, I desperately went seeking for someone that not only had a strong grasp of the written English language (she's a former English Teacher), but also someone I could trust to give me honest feedback about what I created. The interesting thing about this process was that it was the beginning of her journey as an editor. This book was a first for both of us. After numerous revisions, what you have is the finished product, and I could not be prouder of the book or thankful that she had a hand in making a vision a reality. Thank you for all of the time and energy you dedicated to this script. Lakishia is also an author. Her book *Overcome the Obstacle: Pursue the Dream* is a great read that I highly recommend. You can contact her for speaking engagements, her book, and now copyediting at Lakishia@thetapestrynetworkcom.

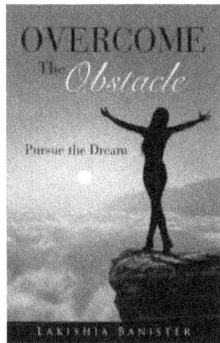

I would also like to thank my wife, Nye, and my son, Mason. This journey hasn't proven very difficult as far as time is concerned, and it was partially due to her giving personality. She was always concerned about my progress in writing, urging me to write more, and was completely supportive when I'd go into "work mode," neglecting other tasks at home. Nothing stopped in our household. This book is a product of a happy home. Mason on the other hand requires lots of attention from me. Occasionally, we had to break our routines in order to get this script completed as well as finish homework daily, study spelling words nightly, read before bed, go to Cub Scouts, and prepare on Tuesdays for Saturday Soccer games. It's the life and I wouldn't have it any other way! I also wrote The M.A.P. with him in mind. I wanted to create something that he could pick up when he was older and refer to if he ever got stuck. It will undoubtedly happen in his lifetime, and if I happen to not be available to help him through a rough patch, I want him to still hear me providing guidance. The one thing that a dad could ever leave his son which is more valuable than inheritance is his

voice in his advice. Mason...you and your future were the catalysts that manifested this book inside of me. Thank you.

I also want to acknowledge my biggest cheerleader, my mother, Dr. Rhonda Hall. When I told her I was writing a personal development book, her exact words were "Well...go for it!" She has always been a go-getter and pushes her kids, family, and friends to be their best. She once told me her line name while rushing Delta Sigma Theta was "Sky." Although I could identify the origin of the name, she proceeded to inform me that her favorite saying and belief was "The Sky is the Limit." She is my lifelong "ecologist" helping me reach higher places so I can fly, and occasionally fall, from the peaks of life all on my own.

About the Author & GOODLIFE!! Coaching

Chester is the Owner and Lead Life Coach of GOODLIFE!! Coaching. He has over fourteen years of experience in the Education field, eleven of those as a classroom teacher and the remainder serving as a Prevention & Intervention Specialist for Accomack County Public Schools. In this capacity, he focuses his efforts on Anti-Bullying, Character Education, encouraging positive student-teacher relationships, mentoring At-Risk Youth, Truancy Prevention, and Threat Assessment. He also is a member of the International Coaching Federation (ICF) and a member of the Black Life Coaches Network (BLC.net).

Chester is a 2001 graduate of Hampton University. He has obtained a Master's Degree in Education Administration from Salisbury University, and earned his Coaching Certification from Academic Life Coaching Inc. He is an avid reader of self-help/leadership books and a diehard gamer. He regularly volunteers his time with Youth Soccer as a Coach and serves as a Parent Leader for Cub Scout Pack 300 in Parksley, VA. He resides on Virginia's Eastern Shore with his wife Nyoka and son Mason.

You can contact Chester for motivational speaking, coaching, or book signing at 757-709-2832 and at chester.hall@goodlife-coaching.com.

GOODLIFE!! Coaching is a life coaching practice that helps individuals realize their vision and accomplish their goals. The company specializes in working with young adults and at-risk adolescents; although they are open to other clients as well. GOODLIFE!! Coaching has a subsidiary brand, BULLYPROOF!! Coaching, which helps elementary and middle school students build life empowerment skills while combating the effects of bullying.

Visit GOODLIFE!! Coaching online at www.goodlife-coaching.com. While there, subscribe to our monthly newsletter, The BLOOPRINT!! You can follow us on Twitter and Periscope @AGOODLIFE and on Facebook at www.facebook.com/g00dlifecoaching. We love getting feedback about what we're doing and hearing about your life changing journeys!

Credits

1. "Celebrities Whose Vision Boards Came True." *Dose of Bliss*. 26 Feb. 2015. Web. 17 Oct. 2015.

2. Gregoire, Carolyn. "This Is Why People Who Live In San Francisco Are So Happy And Healthy." *The Huffington Post*. TheHuffingtonPost.com. Web. 17 Oct. 2015.

3. "How Oprah Used a Vision Board to Envision Barack Obama as President - Johnassaraf.com." *Johnassarafcom*. 5 Nov. 2008. Web. 18 Oct. 2015.

4. "Les Brown Story of Persistence and Preperation." *Ty Bennett RSS2*. Web. 17 Oct. 2015.

5. "Life Lessons." *Life Lessons*. Web. 17 Oct. 2015.

6. "Nawazuddin Siddiqui Thanks Government for Honouring Dashrath Manjhi." *The Indian Express*. 27 Aug. 2015. Web. 17 Oct. 2015.

7. "Story Phoenix." *Story Phoenix*. Web. 17 Oct. 2015.

8. "The Man Who Single-handedly Carved A Road Through a Mountain - Good News Network." *Good News Network*. 21 Mar. 2015. Web. 17 Oct. 2015.

www.ingramcontent.com/pod-product-compliance
Lightning Source LLC
Chambersburg PA
CBHW031518040426
42445CB00009B/286